NAKED ORANGE

POEMS

GABBY BABA

A publication of

Eber & Wein Publishing

Pennsylvania

Naked Orange

Copyright © 2019 by Gabby Baba

All rights reserved under the International and Pan-American copyright conventions. No part of this book may be reproduced, stored in a retrieval system, or transmitted in any form, electronic, mechanical, or by other means, without written permission of the author.

Library of Congress
Cataloging in Publication Data

ISBN 978-1-60880-633-1

Proudly manufactured in the United States of America
by

Eber & Wein Publishing
Pennsylvania

For Alyssa

"I think I'm going through a quarter of a life crisis."
—Anne Reston

CONTENTS

Acknowledgments xi

I.

A Pink Day to Remember 3
Owl Sickness 5
Cattle Cloud Refugee 6
Better Than Destiny 7
Apartment to Sun Dried Air 10
Poem to My Colorful Butterfly 11
Bake a Cake with My Sister 13
A Little Garage for Friends 15
Jackie B Vintage 17
I Found a Necklace 19
Voice of a Venus Flytrap 21
Wacky Love 22

II.

Lock Yourself in a Closet 25
Alive in the Presence of a Dead Fish 28
We Lived in a Box 30
White Teeth 32
I Feel Alone with Us 36
God Is Made of Soup 38
I Had Dreams of Cockatoos and Things 40
Morty and the Birds 42
Python 44
I Only Dance When No One Is Looking 46
Obscenely Anonymous 47
The City Is Ours 48

III.

If I Were Here 51
Naked Orange 53
Hey Anne 55

Hive Minds	56
I Really Love My Girl	57
Paper Light	60
Blue Harpoon	62
Black Irish Taxi Driver	66
Come Here, Monkey	68
Falling Knives and Loud Men	69
Bourbon Smoke and Eyebrows	71
Forever Friend	73

ACKNOWLEDGMENTS

First thanks go to my wonderful parents, Abdallah and Jacqueline Baba. You have always encouraged creativity. I thank you for giving me what your parents couldn't give you. This book is all yours. Shukran.

Thanks to Natalie and George Baba for always being patient with me. It's very unlike me to annoy you both.

Thank you to Suzanne Kawaja for encouraging me to keep writing. I promise I will finish my novel. Just for you.

Thank you to Paul Cobb for being someone I have admired dearly for many years. You are so intelligent and cool and devoted to the ones you love. I promise to take notes.

Thanks to Hannah, Soren, and Julian Cobb for growing up as awesome individuals that I love hanging out with.
Stay cool.

Thank you to Claudia Baba for being a part of this creative process. Your support is incredible. I always enjoy your feedback. And I didn't forget about DeeDee and Majida.

Thanks to Courtney Cathey Chapman for rolling the best blunts.

Thanks to Alyssa DuPree for hating Jesse Eisenberg as much as I do.

Thanks to April DuPree. Just because I adore you.

Thank you to Tori Ortega for always making me laugh.

Thanks to Chiara Lombardi and Andrea Hennekes, for being my second family.

Thanks to Roala and Chloe Baba for being advocate readers.

Thank you to Anne Reston for everything you have done for me. Seriously.

Thanks to Nevena Arsekin and Dina Dubinsky, for being my dearest and oldest friends.

Thanks to JP Denny for all the late night walks. I will always hold a special place for you in my heart.

Thank you to Holly Holloway for all the hospitality.

Thank you to Christina Movaghar for understanding my culture on a level that most people don't get. You only get it when you're in it.

Thank you to Michelle Sanchez for reading my last book. Your kindness is infectious.

Thank you to Shadia Baba, Mimi Baba Zaybak, Fatyn Khawaja Baba, Emily Khawaja Ganim, and Zeena Foteh for all your loving support.

Thanks to Alexis Brooke, for always listening. Nothing defines a person more.

Thanks to Jeanette, Jahanna, and Jannan.

Thank you to Sayed. For all you do.

Deep gratitude to Chandler Vicchio for all your patience, and thank you to the editors and entire staff of Eber & Wein Publishing for giving me this wonderful opportunity.

Finally, grateful acknowledgment to Natalie Del Toro for being my greatest inspiration throughout the years. Your support means more than life itself. Thank you for always being by my side no matter what. Damn, I'm a lucky bitch.

"We envy the luxury: a room to bleed in and break apart."
—Sally Wen Mao

I.

A PINK DAY TO REMEMBER

Here in my billet
I fill my ribs with quartz and amulets.

                    Red feathers swim in my throat.

Now I dance to shed
from her backbone. *I am water*.

                    Unzipping limbo and
                    exposing hostel sheets,

I drank a barrel of mint tea
from the flame of a gut,

                    the gut I carved her name around a
                    hundred and seventy times in the dark.

Wilted and demon flower
lying in the middle of the street,

        is where my life changed.
        I sat next to a lavender escort

diffusing a black scar of smoke
from a moonlike flake,

        escorting my assumptions
        on a pink day.

OWL SICKNESS

The valve is clogged
With no composure.
All will eventually die.
We grieve like machines.
The ones you say you hate,
Are the ones you love.
Like love, I built around you.
That rose stretching towards
A strapless moon,
Blinded by dark matter, is where I gave everything away.
I gave and gave,
To give is to grow,
To grow is to forget.

I am like you,
But brighter.
Stay yourself, fire flower,
Owls sing at night.

CATTLE CLOUD REFUGEE

Sometimes there is no perimeter—

just blankets of sky
scanning the cobalt, dying in the arms
of messages on the back of stars,

ravishing, lolling in the sanctuary,
the old world shore in the hands pressed
between the exhaust button and your thighs.

Sometimes there is no sky—

nothing to choose, to hook mitts around crayons
and frailness, a tiny note in a thimble never read, the
sapphire coat after you've flown, wrinkle and bare,

eight thousand rain droplets spooling green flies,
mulch, a feeding tube, blade and machine—

BETTER THAN DESTINY

Love makes you feel vigorous
In glassy temples

The sun divides our memories
Making love all night to *Drake*

Fucking or dancing
It is all the same

So beautiful
And alive

No one is dying around me
Except for me

Pills I never split
Just your pupils I want to bifurcate

Your posture is the best part of your body

I doubt
anyone has noticed

The scar on your lip is better than fortune
Better than destiny

I want to cut your smile wider
With a knife

While I listen to
The Knife

There is no song to call *"ours"*
No poem that will bring us back

No settling paw
In a painless future

No one will ever know the inside of your hands
Because they are filled with ghostly fumes

I live behind the face of a bonfire
To forget what I have grown to remember

She loved me

And then, notoriously,
She did not

APARTMENT TO SUN DRIED AIR

There is no bread today.
Only jam. Strawberry.
The color delicious. Deceiving.
The anarchy.
To snip the crust
of a jar,
the crepe of a cake—
your prow sinking in her grip,
the slip, the belly flop
into unfamiliar territory.

POEM TO MY COLORFUL BUTTERFLY

        My colorful butterfly,
I tried writing you.
        I don't know where you are.
Tell me you're safe.
        My darling, I was horrible.
Will you forgive me?
        My apology lost its way
        to your front porch.

I disappeared for six years.
        Everything was black.
Even the butterflies.
        I was a black kite.
You are petulant when you drink.
        You're a black kite. Never
        quite free.

I allowed her to disrupt our home.
        I was so stupid.

My voice was bland.
                You left words in my mouth.
I couldn't speak to you.
                I'm not fascinated by
                fascinating people.

I am fascinated by the cartilage
                of a white pelican.
Its overdose wing.
                The saline.
The delicate discomfort
                of cowslip. Eyes heavy, but still safe.

BAKE A CAKE WITH MY SISTER

I will bake a cake with you.

It won't be like saving the world.

There is enough cake for all children.

Some will never get a slice.

Let us pretend that's OK.

Cake will make everyone fat.

I want to be sturdy and slender.

Sculpted like celery.

Almost transparent.

A good taste too quickly is always short-lived.

Like postmodernism.

Your heart, a red velvet flag.

A LITTLE GARAGE FOR FRIENDS

The G Spot was
A naïve horizon.
Laughter and youthful drugs
Occupied by pathological optimism, is where we lived.

When we grow up, we die twice.
I died once already,

The day you left me under the torch.
My lungs
Ingested every sickness,
Every undying secret you painted
On the wall,
Filled with a sound that shook
Like war, we laid on railroad tracks
With one eye open.

I left today
To see my family.

The emporium speaks in riddles,
Bloodlines merge,
Bugs thread like needles in a
Glasshouse sky wounded by neck ties.
The fabric chooses me and ticks the
Proximity, [*the circle of voices*].

I came back today.
My thumb
Against a cold frame,
Maneuvering lips, suggest new ideas.
I am a neighbor to a fugitive,
Disarmed in between
Sprawl and cherry mouth.
It was anxiety,
But beauty.
A dream to get high to,
A second of honesty that felt like a lifetime.

JACKIE B VINTAGE

Dear Mother,

I love your smile
I watched your glamour stitch a
Sidewalk crack
To hold this boring city together
Come float with me
All across the world
Where it is green and blue
Where the sound of wind breaks against a wavelet
As the coral sun melts its arms around
Your pain
Shining on vacant dreams
Then
Filling to the brim of delicate misery

You were a girl lost
In a field of indigo moons
Bursting out yellow petals in the wing

Of a hummingbird brow, *we are hands*
The best shade of green
O to fly free
O to burn free
Like the head of a cigarette resting
On the neck of a retro ashtray
Why love people?
Things are more loyal—a pair of scissors
And a crayon box never abandon
A blank sheet of construction paper

Draw a face with me
Cut it out from this inky,
Cardboard sky
Look up in the clouds
As a plane flies above your head
Reminding you
We couldn't be alone
Even if we wanted to

I FOUND A NECKLACE

To hear you scream
I sense something deep-seated
Whether women love me
Or the idea of me
Expect nothing all at once
I was full of love, but I was dying
I would love to scramble my thoughts
And fry a meal for you
I would love to absorb your body in this sleeping bag
And zip you up tightly, but
Your secrets ate everything in the bedroom
My inadequacy

I found an injured necklace on a chalked sidewalk
The way you found me
While swimming with ugly toads
I'm like a toad, not a frog
I'm not pretty enough to skip

In popularity

I'll never be what others intend
But I will never run away from what
I have not become

VOICE OF A VENUS FLYTRAP

Honey-eaten from bone.
The sun rises over. Assassinating
hurricane. Shrapnel against
an elephant's ribcage,
shrill wind. The plants
I swallow are tender,
a flap in vicious disguise.
Hunger stalks perpendicular to
holograms—snow
falling, the circadian beats,
it listens. And I'm thinking of
kissing her, and how later that night
he patted me on the back
and gave me a beer. His
meaningless voice raped my ear.
I dangled my feet in your empty pool.

WACKY LOVE

For my girl

Here is the moment where we see each other.

This is the opening I have longed for. The gentle caress.

The smell of earth after a hard rain. The sun soaking up

judgment through windows. Our home. The place where

the teachings of a wise woman taught me to be kinder.

What capacity does love have? The burning.

Cottonwood. The burning. Cottonwood.

"I believe in this connection we all have to nature, to each other, to the universe."
—Ada Limon

II.

LOCK YOURSELF IN A CLOSET

I am a windowpane
Pain, pain, pain
I pretend to be poor

On Sundays, a bullet shatters intellect every time
I yell
At a brown feathered face

I left humor on a hanger
My shoulders stalwart
As I watched ruthlessness
Survive

When I hold you
I break into pigments
Of devilish bones and eat a plum
I call out your name as if you are nobody
Wash my face

With a gardenia coated squirrel
As cold rain creeps in
We can't relate
My wings have flames

I tie your shoelaces together in the early morning
To clean around your ankles
I enjoy getting rid of things
More than buying them
To find obscurity
A cryptic butcher hidden in a pocket drawer
A windup doll with a full belly—a fishbone
 Lodged in its throat

I never drink like you

To paint a portrait
Your crestfallen smile, clear as mud,

We are manic

Rescue us, broken child
Recycle this origin
Of living things between us
Bright and dead

ALIVE IN THE PRESENCE OF A DEAD FISH

I had dreamed of conquests wider
> than the beach, watching black skimmers
> > shake their keys and here,

I folded for you with my hands tied behind my back.
> Each part of me the mouth of an electrical
> > storm, and your green eyes

flooded my heart—
> *above, around, and within*, billowing in the
> > breed of ripples. I felt the spark of

your skin, tongue of a swelling sea,
> the bones in my knees exploded shells,
> > shook like bees,

and I think the last time we danced, I readjusted
        my collar, the back of my neck
            seemed to hum

when you grabbed me closer—*the way you*
      did years before
        when we walked forth

a trail beneath the quarter-moon.
      And there in that abandoned road,
        I will imagine

the creak of your bedchamber, engulfed
      in the cavity underneath your brow,
        wounded window stuffed

and sewed, suggesting I should have taken
      you home that night to trace a seam in between
        our lungs along the dimple, blue earth.

WE LIVED IN A BOX

Orange corals surrounded our feet
Feathers fell from mountain tops
Carving out whale sounds
And nonsense
I built a fort in my living room as an adult
Ghetto rises in movies
The kind of thing I am waiting for
I don't watch films like I used to
I listen to the story of a waterfall
The beauty and innocence
Between day and night
When blinks are silent
Like a promised virgin
Contaminated by abandonment
Where a dizzy river appears behind a closed door,
Your finger in the hinge

The room had many openings

An air mattress floating in a bottle
Of honey
Of Irish whiskey
Where we slept in our clothes
And tap danced
In metallic slippers

Growing up with
Soft outlines of heaven and porn,
I rather see the world through a window
Through poetry
The poetry that rewrote our sins
We screamed as if walls could talk back
Confused
Trying to understand
Why is listening the most difficult chore? Tell me,
Why is space door less?

WHITE TEETH

I'm skinny now, but that doesn't matter.

To hate anything more than sandpaper, you can
always spot the red-tailed fox. I will bury tears,

all the tears, all the damp smoke between my fingers.
What I kept as a lonely child.
I want to be like you and fuck like

the gods. And murder all the animals
to show them how I feel

body becoming firework,
body becoming illness.

In spite of it all, I speak pain.
I speak loudly for mature women.

She woke up next to me,

told me to listen up.

My cartoon mouth doesn't speak.
My hair, a black origami parachute. Like a mulberry tree.

She tells me what to do and
yells a creature's name

as I hammer in a different direction.
I could murder furniture right now.

                                                                           She is a professor.
Drinks red wine with a straw. I don't like clutter either.

She says,
as long as you smile you can fuck whoever you want.
You fuck with rage, but your skin is so soft.

Eat up the power [of] contrast.
Know what you look like matters, Gabrielle.

I had never been alive in this institution

like the ex-smoker. *I drew blood religiously.*
I want to tie floss around my neck to
hang on my insecurities,

to look in a mirror, to smile back—
the only thing that gets me laid.

I will grin every time,

I will grin every time

I floss before midnight,
and maybe you should too.

If you don't, someone will taste
awfulness.

I want these teeth when I'm eighty,
to look back at my children's children.

I want these teeth when I'm ninety,
so when you kiss me,

you still taste
sweetness.

I can't spend the night at your house, sweet angel.
Do you have floss in your bathroom drawer?

I floss religiously,
(Unwaxed Dental Floss)

after I watch T.V.,
after I play basketball,
after I eat a juicy peach,
tu   lips,   like you.

I FEEL ALONE WITH US

It's a lonesome world
Of course I want children
What else is there to live for?
I'll never have kids the way you do
Half of me/half of her
It's a tragedy to be gay
I don't see pride
To be cold
Like a fingerless glove
To eat crackers and snort blow off your tits, O
We are
The chokehold of this continent
A submarine with cranny windows
No, a bleeding pomegranate with feline eyes
My cat meows and meows
To play fetch at six
In the morning

Yes, cats can fetch

Babies aren't as talented
Only in their opinions

GOD IS MADE OF SOUP

It was a sad day
It was sad watching my mother among the nuns
Like the exact same way I felt shame
When I caught my wife looking through my journals
Most things that hold people together
Have nothing to do with love

There are ways to cut mirrors
To make up canvases of light
To hang in catholic churches
      Is there only one way to look at a painting?

A thousand places, we are not the same
A thousand and one places, we are
The way we keep our spouses sterile
I hate elitists
I know I won't amount to anything
Anything at all
Especially in this sexless body

But you still loved me

  You're a waxy soul

I was bored most of the time, but I still

Run for you

My face, a silver amalgam

Showing you

I eat soup with my fingers too

I HAD DREAMS OF COCKATOOS AND THINGS

I had a dream about you
For many years I believed
I was more than scum
But I wasn't more
Than a girl who wanted to run away from
A perfect life

I had loved a man
He died
But I left long before
When I was a kid
When I was vile

I never expected my father's acceptance
But I was stupid enough
To demand acknowledgment

Beau, I find your tenderness annoying
Most of the time
Build a kingdom and I *will* be king
Play chess and I will *kill* the king
I bluffed many rounds
We all
Have been cheated on
Hate to tell you
That's the only true blue story

We all will drag
Across a splinter deck in
Corduroy shirts
To watch cockatoos smoke serrano peppers
As they imitate millionaires in
Pink leather suits
I had loved a cockatoo

MORTY AND THE BIRDS

He talks to himself

        But his words are valued

People think he is strange

        I don't want to be a weirdo

I want to be angelic

        Always looking to the right, *a goat*

No wait, *a swan*

        Colored by a child

I know half the world is dead

        Dug inside the inner sun as it set

It was silent

    Full of purple feathers

When I saw the moon rise

    It exploded in many voices

Like youth, *I swallowed*

    Like love, *I contained*

Me, a rainbow quill: grenade confetti

    You, wild star, disappearing

Behind orange curiosity

PYTHON

I was a mother once. All of a sudden, I wasn't.
        I know you love him or her and the
                aquarium. And don't love me.

I don't think you love anything but the events.
        There is hail, the odorless terra,
                and life made of dead things.

Live things are bluish black. I stomp on anything
        I can to get to, *awake*. I am afraid
                of living things:

the stroke of velvet hands, callous war
        crushing the walls of film strips,
                paper ash terrace collapsing on

newborn laughter.
        Identification by barefoot
                is where I slumbered,

under the stairwell next to the cob rollers,
> bed sores from your marble-smooth
>> nape. To get to you is to squeal

in the explosion of a wildfire, rutted wilderness
> when birds close their beaks, the credence
>> of incubus, tiny weak lamp—

the land I gave up.

We learn that nothing stays, everything splits.

The body I gave up

I ONLY DANCE WHEN NO ONE IS LOOKING

in the petal of
        a crease, the under sleep of a drape.

                beyond *the sullen mist*,
                      flowers bleed   from

inside-out metaphors,

                blooming   hail,
                          pirouetting

in fuchsia heels.
        pills. pills. pills.

                the absence of gravity
howls and howls,
                      even if I'm not here.

OBSCENELY ANONYMOUS

When the door opened the empyrean diverged

    And those afternoons my hands opened

In a villa of purple tiles, peacock blue roofs,

    A ghost lantern with letters sealed

In the bottom of its fuel bottle

    The retina of a wondering sea covered

By winter sheath

    Collecting sawdust in the salty night

Paddock dissolving in the background behind white

    And us, luminous luminous luminous

THE CITY IS OURS

        Where do you keep your sharp tools?
        We can change evolution.
        The city is ours.

Where do you keep all the keys you stole?
We can leave and never come back.
The city is ours.

        Why do you always carry a dog chain with you?
        You can't bring that in the car.

The city is yours.
The city is yours.
The city is yours.

"Freedom is not contentment. Freedom is only art."
—Dorothea Lasky

III.

IF I WERE HERE

If I were here gilt-edged
with you never returning
I wouldn't have
cremated your letters, here and now,

specter cinders feeding toddlers at
the poolside, lifeguards doing what

they don't do. I can't recall the last morning
when we were in sync, not really—the phantom
limb is there but not:

a finger: an oversize pellet
a leg: a hollow vent
a torso: a cannon
a head: a cannonball
an eye: *the button*—somewhere
in the monastic a lama whispers
a secret message in my ear

and I retreat, stripping the bed alone
to reconcile.

NAKED ORANGE

Over there where we cross paths,
Real things are camouflaged.
I learn to be fluorescent,
And it's because of you.

I know we tend to hide
Under umbrellas next to the ones
We want to protect.
O how
Caring is only defined by action, and
You are action, my love.
Overflowing under a mosaic lamp,
Sound stops,
And we dissolve in conversation.

                        Your intimacy is genuine.

Only you can lead your destiny.
Don't sacrifice your worth and
Dissipate behind a costume

For the ones who don't clothe you.

Part of me already knew

I could be more than a gesture—your sunshade tree,

The leaves, the pigment, the undertone,

~~Haiku~~. The bitter to your sweetness.

HEY ANNE

Electricity between bodies
    can be found anywhere.

Chemistry between minds, well,
    I can only count on one hand for that.

My dear, I supply you with gold in both my hands.
    I think you're much rarer than a diamond,
        a silent daydream.

I can be a hazardous slope,
    a property measuring control on wetter days.

I tend to love when there is nothing left *to* love.

Listen to me, sweet angel.
    Stay clear from the maelstrom of inamoratas,
    especially a woman who abandons womanhood—
        he is not fooling anyone but *herself.*

HIVE MINDS

Chirp a whisper in tiny pockets.

A muddy whale crosses inky footprints.

Invite flamingos. *Invite vapor*.

      Stuck to the wing. Of a swollen rainbow.

Take the stairs.
You'll end up in the same place.

Circle.
Sphere.
      A dose.
      Sleep.
Circle.
Sphere.
      A dose.   Sleep.

I REALLY LOVE MY GIRL

I love our home
That picture hanging

Reminds me of everything
I've hung onto

Yes, I have loved people
And red lipstick

Yes, I gave all of me and kicked pink bunnies
All around your feet

You have to know
The past is filled with many faces

But you are much more compelling
Because you stayed

Stuffing red roses
In blue branches

You punctured the heartbeat
Of my wound

And washed my organs white
My lungs, hearty on the kitchen counter

Your heart glowing
Like an autumn wreath

A yellow ribbon spewing
Under the surging sea

To put back together the whispers
Of a broken crest

Tie my vertebrae to this passageway
Attach a note saying,

DIVORCE: NOT PENDING

PAPER LIGHT

In every photograph
I am an old lady

The shape of a modest star
To be with you in dreams

In the waiting room
I call out for you

Breast-stroking in
Scarlet welkin

The back of your wave
Colors spew curtains

Neon conversation
Until I couldn't speak red

That place where we lived, *we bargained*
The thin hiss of

Mummified cobwebs,
Circus and jealousy

Filling up to the hem
Of disappointment

I suspect the rope is lubricated
By the crawling spill tide

The duchess, toehold,
Serpent snarling in the vestibule

Take your finger out
From the outlet, night child

I caught you making animal sounds
To a block of moldy cheese

BLUE HARPOON

For Courtney

We only listen to *Florence and the Machine* when we are
Stoned out of our minds.

Do you remember *Portishead?*
We flew all the way to New Jersey
To touch the hand of *Beth Gibbons*.
The universe was alive,
The way the past felt when we
Rolled fat blunts in the barn.
We spoke in poise vocabulary
As though our education meant something.

O did we sacrifice,
To sacrifice is to be malleable. I disagree.
I have realized the trust in shadows.
I never ate and slept on empty roads.
A false sense,

A real sense   of *being*.

Now I am sober.
I see the world not in my books,
But with ordinary eyes.
We drank Red Bull for breakfast
To perform for them.
Abuse equals salience.

I always learn more from bodily rejection.

To sing and fuck,
To animate the stars inflicted on me,
I have yet to find a face as bright as rubies.
I forget names all the time,
And if you look close enough, all faces start
To look the same.
After all, I am not dead, but
I know they are no more alive.
I forget my voice at home most days and
Walk pass miracles all the time.
I never thought

I could swim across the Atlantic
With my breath held the entire way.
But I realize, love is not just another word for death.
To talk *of* things is not to *be* of things.

This is what I know to be
Under the green shade,

This is what I know to be
Under the black rail,

Where the train conductor
Composes a left-handed switch

To dump gold cobras
In miniature coal baskets,

Where the grey-tailed captain
Sinks with his ark,

As the ship crew hang on the tuft
Of a moth's wing.

This is what I know to be
Under the cape of a porcelain ballerina.

I lied many times
In a blindfolded alley and
Borrowed knives for amusement.
My cheeks barren.
Now I want to be worthy of the boondocks.
A permanent caretaker
Of a pouring sea.
Your honesty, *the weight of skin*,
Soothing the bitter taste of those
We have loved.

Then you emerged and
belonged anew.

To someone—
Little *Willow*,
A blue harpoon.

BLACK IRISH TAXI DRIVER

His friend ruined his body for the world of women.
To be unrestricted, requiem burns.

The night terrors beetle—wearing underpants, rotted
teeth, spindrift nosebleed punctured
        from orphans.

        A rollick of carbonated storm erases turnpikes.
Waste in the liver, clone rumors in the thorax,
a gold pendant blown out like a
              vellum candle.

        Headed northward with chalked palms,
        his beastly chuckle, *he lives like a king*, he says.

Stray dogs sleep cold and wet.

It stays chilly here, I pray for forgiveness.
        Here are my bloodstone sandals.

My father had forty-seven children and nine wives—
                smashup elbows, empty pockets.
He lives in a cave.

        If you smell, you pay taxes.
            I don't smell anymore.

My mother carried berries and wood on top of her head.
She was obedient. She elevates like boiling tea in its
    magnetic umbra—*keep your eyes close to the ground,*
    know the atrium has boundaries.

COME HERE, MONKEY

You are the milky brew.

Hold my breasts to your breasts, then take me.

I think it is cute you have a puppy.

I think it is sweet that you call him Monkey.

Come here, Monkey.

I will hold you close to my chest like

Your lost mother once did.

FALLING KNIVES AND LOUD MEN

For Shadia

How come when our fathers speak,
People think they are mad?
I tell my friends that is how they talk.
They yell. Their voices are stern,
Their language is aggressive.
I find humor in the families
That communicate collectively.
Where we live,
Most things are never said.
Where we live,
Compromise is nothing more than an image.

I know how hard it is to live up
To the traditional minds
That constantly surround us.
It doesn't bother me like it did when I was young.

If anything, cousin, I have learned
To step down from the fight.
I don't keep a knife in my pocket anymore.
This is our family. This is loyalty.
This is fucking love.
And I know we have one thing in common,
To want to make them proud of who we are,
Who they want us to be.

BOURBON SMOKE AND EYEBROWS

Half-skinned behind a blind, the girl could be
>anyone but it's my sister.

Last night there was a bile man who thirsts for
>dark skin and dark hair. *Aphotic zone.*

He stuffs parachutes and bourbon rumors
>in eggshells—*her electric
>shadow somersaults.*

What language do you speak? What do you say
>in the ears of your lovers?

He washed his mouth with detergent and slit the
>bark carefully. *The wires thread.*

She ducked in the left wing behind a delphinium—
        laid like a bone, blossoming.

FOREVER FRIEND

I filled up a hot-air balloon with resentment &
    drifted away. I fell hopeless without notice,

for the blessings of dark water. I took pictures of fog
    while you slept in a room filled   of empty frames.

Your pulse, fractured. Your promise, bruised.
    You took a crowbar to my chest & crushed it

wide open. A sound of *stillness* broke in me; the
    gathering of dead moths dispersed pieces of rib

like glitter lost. A typewriter sat at the bottom of a lake.
    I begged. *I can behave. Sorry, I am closed. Entirely.*

I cried, *rewrite me*. Take out all the parts that made her leave.
    I constantly   sharpen my teeth for a changing beast.

If I were to leap from a silo, if I belong to anything anymore,
    it is the surgical wind inside you that makes me itch.

Our affair is never the romance I imagine.
    Half bored.   Half fascinated.

You've become a careless lover & I've become
    an amateur conversationalist.

Don't make me a chapter in your book you keep flipping
    back to. Don't be the paper-thin blade pressed against

my breastbone.   I crushed a handful of pills
    to make plaster with all your thoughtless

mistakes in hand, so when I coil around your throat,
    I am molding you—

you come back smaller every time.
    This is how I learn to transform an arm into a wing.

I never mistake what I love for what I lose.

You're always in love over & over again.

One day you will lose count like the countless times you
    find yourself back in these emulsified arms of mine.

I stop questioning why my bones   pulsate like butterflies.
    I stop questioning why you keep coming back.

I watched you put your ear to the ice of a skating rink: skulls
    spying through every crevice of your perfect skin;

We know how you like to be fucked.
    I want to massacre all of your lovers & build a

residence with their bones—light a match & watch each
    composure burn while I strip your skin bare like a

naked orange. Nothing kills faster than the impact of glass,
    nothing kills faster than your clothes off.

Bodies will lie, but never the way a memory will.
    This is why I like to remain in the blankness of a

canvas, to be the buffered jawbone polished by language.
    I am the motherland that will invade your harvest &

morph you silent. You only know what I let you know.
    When I grieve, *I reveal things.*

I watched a blind boy carry his newborn brother across a river
    as rain became sea. A girl face down in mud.

Her mother ran inside to get vinegar. He gave money.
    I explored faces & prayed that night to not dream,

to never dream again, for nightmare is all I will ever be.
    Come visit me far from here,

in the far darkness of jade—a region in disposable to light
    where head separates from   body.

Slide down this mercury chute with embroidery nails.
    Fill your hands with culture, but caution,

for my hands are as empty as the pages in my journal.

Say you will meet me there,

in that grunge habitat we once shared holding a decade
    spent carving octaves in each other's backs,

so when there is nothing left to say,
    we will have found a way to sing.

Say you will come,
    live in this last moment *in the death of us*—

liberate your enslavement from a pendulum clock before the
    revolution   beneath your feet has

only one train station left.
    Say you will   wait for   me.

ABOUT THE AUTHOR

Gabby Baba holds a B.S. in Psychology from the University of Houston and is the author of *The Sullen Mist* and *Even If I'm Not Here*. Her work has appeared in the publications *This Time Around: Anchors Aweigh, Best Poets of 2015,* and *American Poet*. In 2016, her second poetry collection was featured at the national BookExpo America (BEA) in Chicago. She currently lives in Houston.

www.ingramcontent.com/pod-product-compliance
Lightning Source LLC
Chambersburg PA
CBHW022122040426
42450CB00006B/808